The author asserts written by him in th digital or audio forı parts of this book in any format must be approved by the publisher P&P Press.

Published by P&P Press

28 Habost Port of Ness, Isle of Lewis
Scotland HS2 0TG

Copyright 2017

We All Flew Over the Cuckoos Nest

By

Ron Coleman

Acknowledgements

I have many people to thank for writing this book so if your name is not here it is an oversight and I apologize in advance.

I need to thank my wife Karen and the kids who have put up with my swinging moods while I have been writing, They have listened to the stories contained in this book over and over again without them it would never have gotten finished.

I also want to thank the staff at the coronary care unit at   hospital in Perth Australia whose skill and dedication saved my life I cannot thank them enough their skill wrote much of this book with me.

To Mike Smith Paul Baker and John Jenkins whose friendship and time spent eating good food and drinking fine ale and telling tales set up many of these stories.

To John Mickey, Sharon, Katrina and others from HVN Manchester without whom I would never got out of the starting blocks.

For Terry and Julie and their family who helped me through the worst of times not forgetting Marius and Sandra they are to blame.

Dedicated

To

Mary & Ronnie

(Mum and Dad)

Introduction

We all flew over the cuckoos nest is not a book in the traditional sense rather it is a collection of stories most of them true some embellished and some adapted from other not related fields about the psychiatric system. Whilst the book is intended to be funny it is not in anyway attempting to minimize the real pain and suffering that those who have been or are in the psychiatric system go through.

Though no doubt some will find my attitude to having a laugh about mental health disturbing I cannot find it in myself to apologise to them as I am sure many will have never used or been used by mental health services and will judge me on the basis of a political correctness that whilst talked about often enough in mental health is rarely practiced on those who receive services.

Having spent many years in acute psychiatric wards as a patient I remember that most of the discussions between us happened in the smoking room (yes we were allowed to smoke indoors at this time). We would often tell stories of things that had happened to us both in hospital and in the community. Some of these stories were sad, some were challenging but many were funny. This fun is often lost in the system that focuses on risk and illness rather than on health and opportunity.

We all flew over the cuckoos nest is also my personal up yours statement to everything I hate about psychiatry from the arrogance of a lot of psychiatrists to the use of detention pin down, seclusion and ECT as ways of enforcing control over people who have committed no crime yet are often treated as criminals.

This for me is the real madness it is a system gone mad. My response is therefore to laugh at our stories I will no longer live in fear of what might be but rather enjoy what is.

I hope readers will laugh with me and visualize these stories from the dog Fido at the beginning of the book to the car driver at the end of the book but more than anything else I hope readers will learn to laugh at their own moments of madness

Ron Coleman May 2017

Contents

1 Fido

2 I forgot my Medication

3 Him Next Door

4 The football

5 The ward the smoke room and the ward round

6 Watching cricket with the police

7 The psychiatrist' the plant and the windowsill

8 The Conference (Adapted)

9 leave your libido at the door

10 Taking Nurses for a walk

11 The Courtyard

12 DSM is it printed by Marvel comics? Because! It is funny

13 Victor and the mobile phone

14 Christmas in the psychiatric unit

15 Shorts

16 The Schizophrenic Rat and Other Tales

17 The things they said

18 To John Williams Funny man

19 Diagnosing the blues

20 To parents and other inner critics

21 More Shorts

22 The househusband journals

23 Crofters Diary

24 The baby, the shape box and the mallet

25 The Wizard of OZ

26 An Anonymous Tip

27 Turnaround

1 Fido (Anon)

"They said I was Mad I said they were mad Dam them they outnumbered me" (Nathaniel Lee Restoration Poet)

This first story is very short and I heard it a long time ago whilst sitting in the smoking room in some psychiatric unit in London, the story is set in another psychiatric unit near Dundee called Liff Hospital and it goes something like this.

In the early 1950's one of the long stay patients at the hospital would often wander the grounds of Liff hospital with a tin can tied to a piece of string. He would walk this tin can as if it was a dog, indeed he even called the tin can Fido in fact truth be told he was convinced the tin can was a dog called Fido.

One day as he was walking Fido around the grounds he saw two psychiatrists walking towards him. As he was passing them one of the psychiatrists asked how he was. "Fine" was his reply. The psychiatrist who had asked the question winked at his colleague, looked at the patient, and then to the tin can and said "well jack I'm glad to hear that and how is your dog Fido doing this fine summers day" Jack looked at Fido then at the Doctor and replied "oh come on Doctor don't be so daft anyone can see that, that is not a dog it's a tin can on a piece of string" Jack then walked off.

The two Doctors remained where they were watching Jack stroll on pulling the tin can behind him. "Well Paul" said the first "Jack seems to be making real progress". "Aye David" replied the second doctor it seems like the medication is finally beginning to work". Nodding happily to each other they continued on their way back to the hospital building.

Meanwhile Jack was still wandering around with his tin can on its piece of string after another few minutes he stopped looked down at the tin can with affection in his eyes and said "Well Fido we fooled them that time eh"

Enough said.

2 I forgot my Medication

I can't for the life of me remember where I first heard the following story but like many of the stories in this collection it is true and its truth is the challenge that many of us will have to face like it or not.

It is the late 1950's and the introduction of a new drug is being touted as the greatest advance in the treatment of schizophrenia, this new wonder treatment is a drug called chlorpromazine. Hospitals all over the world start trying this drug with patients who are in back wards. In a New York psychiatric hospital it was decided to try the new drug on a number of people in the long stay ward.

One of the men (lets call him Bill) was selected to try chlorpromazine as a last resort. Bill had been on a long stay ward for many years and was seen as a hopeless case, he was given the drug and was continually observed and interviewed as to how he was doing. It seemed to Bill that everyone in the hospital was now interested in him. After only a few days, staff started to notice extraordinary changes in Bill, he was becoming much more active, talking more and engaging in creative pursuits such as art (something that he had done before he came into the psychiatric system). So impressed with his progress the hospital managers decided to buy him an easel, paintbrushes and oil paints.

Within a few weeks Bill was moved from his long stay locked ward into a newly built open ward. On this ward Bill was given more freedom, more choice, more time, more paint and even more monitoring and interviews. Still he continued to improve his artwork was now sought after by people outside of the system. He became much more socially aware and was fast becoming a cause célèbre for a number of the staff who were sure that he should no longer be kept in hospital.

The doctors responsible for his treatment agreed and they started making plans for his discharge. Bill started going out of the hospital at first with staff and then on his own. The time out on his own was extended and every time he returned staff would interview him keeping detailed records on his continuing progress. As plans for his discharge developed, a house was found for him to live Independently in, support was organized to help him settle in and maintain his house.

The doctors were astounded by his progress they now had a treatment that worked on up to now hopeless cases of schizophrenia. They made the decision to finally discharge Bill and set a date, everyone at the hospital was ecstatic.

The day finally arrived and Bill went round all the staff thanking them for their help, Bill then went back to his room to pack his few belongings. The doctors came to say their goodbyes and wish him well, then it was time for him to go, he walked slowly through the ward for the last time carrying his belongings in a little backpack. Staff walked with him to the door to say their final farewells, on reaching the door Bill stopped and thought for a moment. Suddenly in a fairly loud and panicky voice he said to one of the staff "here hold my bag I've bloody well forgot something.

Bill rushed back to his room followed by one or two members of staff on getting back to his Room Bill lifted the mattress off his bed and removed an old sock. He left the room and headed back to the door sock in hand and staff still following him. He asked for his bag back and once it was handed over one of the staff asked him " what's the sock for Bill" Bill pulled the sock inside out over his now opened backpack and out fell the tablets that staff thought he had been taking for the last few months and said in a serious voice "I forgot my medication" Now there's a thought.

3 Him Next Door

Like a lot of people with mental health problems, my life would get really difficult when my neighbors' found out about my mental health status. I have lived in houses where people upon finding out I was a mental health patient have smashed my windows or broken down my front door and robbed what little I had.

I also found myself often being housed in hard to let houses, where you felt isolated and afraid much of the time. I did however live in a couple of shared houses that were really nice I even lived in one with a garden that I could sit in during summer. It is in the nice house where the following story all of it true I hasten to add takes place.

During my career as a psychiatric patient I spent a lot of my time escaping from psychiatric units I particularly would escape on a Thursday mainly because it was the day I was paid my pension and would therefore have money to spend. When people have asked me what is the significance of this I often reply by telling them that it proves one thing about me and that is "I might have been mad but I was never stupid"

On this particular escapade I had escaped from hospital on the Thursday afternoon, spent the evening with friends and went home late at night and had a good nights sleep. The following morning was gloriously warm so I decided to sit in my garden with a cup of tea and a book and lap up the suns' rays.

As I was sitting there he appeared the neighbor from hell, he did not like me and I did not like him. He also knew I was a psychiatric patient and treated me as if I had an IQ of 20. Our gardens did not have a fence between them, so he came skulking over to me and said, "oh they have released you again have they?" "Nah I replied I've done a runner". He looked a bit shocked at that and retorted, "should you not get yourself back to the hospital" "nah I'm not going back" I shot back at him. He then spent the next few minutes making small talk then he told me he was going inside to get a drink and would be right back. I knew exactly what he was going to do; He was going indoors to telephone the police and tell them that I had escaped from a psychiatric unit and was currently sitting in the garden in some bizarre state. When he gave the police my name they would no doubt after a quick check of their records realize he was telling the truth and come and get me.

Unperturbed by any of this I continued to sit reading my book and sipping my tea, neighbor from hell reappeared with a cold drink some five minutes later and continued to chat to me. Ten minutes later I saw the police car coming round the corner, they pulled up outside the house and the car doors opened and out came two policemen. As they walked towards my house I got up and walked towards them, when we came together I quietly spoke to the officers saying "are you here for Ron Coleman" "yes" the one nearest to me replied "that's him over there" I said pointing to neighbor from hell "thanks" came the reply and they strode purposely towards him.

On reaching the neighbor one of the officers told him that he had to come with them, he looked at the officers in astonishment spluttering and pointing at me saying "that's the one you want" then almost at screaming pitch "he's Ron Coleman you bloody idiots" he continued at this point I spoke to the policemen in a quiet, calm voice and nodding knowingly said "oh dear he always says things like that" at this my neighbor went ballistic shouting and swearing at the police who started almost carrying him to the car eventually getting him there they put him in the back one of the officers with him. The other officer calmly walked around to the drivers seat got in and drove off with him next door.

I hasten to add that he did not remain my next-door neighbor for long for some reason the powers that be decided I should move.

4 The football

I always found consultant psychiatrists to be a strange breed with little or no sense of humor. One psychiatrist I had was a really intense guy who even after knowing him for two years I had never seen him smile. I remember one session I had with him where we were talking about my suicidal feelings.

All professionals are a bit weird when you talk about suicide but psychiatrists especially so, it is probably to do with their legal responsibilities and that if anything happens to you it is them that has to go before the coroner and try to explain what has happened. So in one sense you can understand their almost obsessional state about suicide.

So picture the scene I am in the interview room with my doctor and he has been quizzing me about how I am feeling so I tell him that I often waken up in the morning wishing I were dead. He asks me did I want to die I replied that I often wanted to die. He ponders this for a few seconds and then asks me how would I kill myself.

Right at that moment my voices start up and one voice in particular starts talking "what do you call a psychiatrist on a football field" it says " I don't know" I replied to myself not speaking out loud because I am in the interview room with the psychiatrist and didn't want him to know my voices were speaking to me "the ball" says the voice.

I burst out laughing at this moment and my doctor started to scribble in my notes. He never once asked my why I was laughing he just looked at me with that serious face he had perfected and to all intention purposes totally ignored what had happened.

Many years later I got access to my notes and this was what the psychiatrist had written about this incident. "MR Coleman was laughing when we were discussing suicide this is consistent with his diagnoses of schizophrenia" and in brackets beside this statement he had written (inappropriate affect). All because of a ball on a football field!

5 The ward the smoke room and the ward round

Psychiatric wards are strange places on numerous occasions I was told by social workers that I needed to go into the psychiatric hospital for a rest. I might have believed that the first time I went into a psychiatric unit but really! Can you imagine getting much of a rest in a ward full of people who are all distressed at the same time? I think not.

The other strange thing about the ward is the lack of staff on the ward, for some reason most staff are needed in the office no one can tell us why but that is the place the system thinks that staff are most helpful to psychiatric patients. They do important things in the office such as writing notes about patients explaining in wondrous detail how the patient is feeling that day, what the patient is planning to do in the next day and even what the patient has been thinking about.

All of these amazing insights are written in the patients' notes without the staff member ever leaving the office or talking with the patient. I remember when I first got access to my notes how horrified I was with what the staff had written about me then I got angry with some of the incredible things they thought I was thinking then finally I just laughed at their foolishness.

My laughter happened as I was comparing their notes with a journal that I was keeping and there it was in black and white. My quiet weekend on the ward, on this particular weekend according to my notes I was cooperative, good humored, and thoughtful. According to my journal however I was not even on the ward I was on home leave from the Friday until the Sunday. The ward can sure be a strange place to be or even not to be depending on whom you ask. (Surely too much Descartes?)

Now in my days on the psychiatric ward there was one oasis of tranquility, a place of safety if you will, a place where one could relax and be at one with oneself, the name of this asylum was of course the smoke room. This room was a ward within the ward a place of healing where peer support has its true roots within psychiatric services.

In this inner sanctuary of wisdom we would gather patients all and discuss the reality of our beliefs compared to the absurdity of the systems beliefs. We would often find things amusing and would laugh loudly together and our discussions were mostly wide-ranging and intelligent though they could also be bizarre and nonsensical in other words within the smoke room we were normal.

That of course was until any member of staff invaded our space, as soon as that happened our smoke room would become a very different place the noise of laughter and conversation would be replaced by silence. We would sit there, all looking at the floor saying nothing looking desperate, depressed, dejected and distraught. The member of staff would often ask if everybody was okay to which we would mumble some kind of reply that would appear to keep the member of staff happy, as they would go from whence they came. As soon as they left the room our conversations and laughter would recommence.

If the smoke room was where all the talking really happened; the ward round was a place for the surreal. This was the domain of the doctor it was here where important decisions were made things like whether you could go out to the shops on your own, or go home on weekend leave or even spend sometime in the grounds without being escorted. The ward round had the feel of a courtroom around it, with the doctor playing Judge, Jury, and prosecutor all that was missing was the white wig. There was a silly sort of game that was played out in the ward round I called it "home or stay" it was my game and the doctor played whether he or she wanted to or not.

There is really only one important rule to this game and that is you have to decide if its home or stay before you go into the ward round if you decided it was stay before you entered the room the object of the game was to get kept in hospital. In many ways getting kept in hospital was fairly easy as there were a number of gaming gambits that could be used. These included:

1. The voices are getting worse.
2. I wish I were dead.
3. Are you a member of the secret service disguised as a doctor?
4. There is nothing wrong with me.
5. Total silence.
6. Shouting loudly at the doctor.

Normally a combination of two or more of the above would ensure that I would be kept in hospital until at least the next ward round. If however the object of the game was home you would use a different set of strategies normally in response to the main question asked by the doctor, The conversation would go something like this.

Psychiatrist "well Ronald you have been here for a little while now, are you still hearing voices?

Me "it's funny you should mention that they are still around but much quieter it's like mumbles in the distance"

Psychiatrist "that's good"

Me "yeah it's brilliant I feel I can think again much more myself if you know what I mean?

Voice 1 "you've never had a thought in your life ya daft numpty"

Voice 2 "How is he (the psychiatrist) going to know what you mean when you don't know what your talking about yourself Coleman you bam-pot"?

Psychiatrist " That's wonderful Ron so tell me how's your mood?"

Me "oh it's really good I feel so much better now, thanks to the team here"

Voice 1 "oh it's really good I feel so much better now, thanks to the team here you're a bloody creep Coleman"

Voice 2 "feeling better; thanks to the team; this lot couldn't play we themselves, you're talking the piss so you are"

Voice 1 "I'll give you feeling better once we're out of here, I'm going to take you apart bit by bit."

Psychiatrist " Good has anybody else got anything to say about how Ron is getting on"?

OT "Ron has been really active in the groups the past few days, I mean getting involved in discussions and talking very positively about the future"

Voice 1 "you have been a busy Coleman haven't you, in discussions as well, talking shit more like"

Nurse " we have observed a big change in the attitude that Ron has to the nursing staff. He does not appear to be angry with us any more"

Voice 2 to the tune of the wall " We don't need no medication, we don't need no thought control, nurses paid just to detain us; Hey doctors! Leave us guys alone"

By this stage I am sitting in the room humming the No More Bricks in the Wall to myself, and thinking about Pink Floyd, the doctor gives me one of those knowing looks and says:

Doctor " Well Ron do you think your ready to go home?"

Voice 2 " I thought he was the doctor why is he asking you?"

Voice 1 "He's a quack his first name is Donald and his second name is Duck. Get it?

Ron to the voices "shut up smart ass" to the doctor "now that you've said it yes I do think it is time for me to go home".

Doctor "okay Ron shall we say home on Thursday"

Ron "cool"

Voice 2 "Game, set and match to Coleman"

Ron to voices "Thank guys"

The moral of this tale is simple "nothing is never as it appears" and in psychiatry this is certainly true.

6 Watching cricket with the police

As I stated earlier in the book escaping from hospitals was for me an essential requirement for every POW (Patient On Ward). The following story is a very true account of one of my escapes, which I first told at a conference in Liverpool, organized by the Merseyside police.

At the time the story happened I was detained in a hospital in Manchester and it was well into summer. I had been in hospital for a few weeks and was getting bored so I decided it was time for a night out. (I had not been allowed out on my own since my admission a not uncommon position for me to be in) My usual nights out (escapes) were either Thursday or Friday mainly because I was paid on Thursday but sometimes did not get out to collect my money till Friday because staff were busy.

This was one of those weeks bang in the middle of the summer holidays lots of staff on holidays so it was a Friday before I walked to the shops accompanied as usual by two members of staff that looked like a pair of heavies from some gangster movie. After getting my money buying a pack of cigs we returned to the ward.

The art of escaping is about biding your time waiting for the right moment and then going before anyone notices and summer is a great time for escaping as the saying goes opportunity indeed comes to those who wait. Well today was not going to be a long wait, too many staff on holiday lots of agency staff that did not know their ass from their elbow when it came to the ward I was on.

I waited until half the staff went for their break, the rest were busy and the one left in the office next to the ward door was an agency nurse who did not know me from Adam. I put my jacket on and walked passed the door looked into the office and said " thanks a lot Ron is sleeping at the moment I will come back to see him tomorrow" with that I smiled waved and walked out. I walked quickly out of the hospital hailed a taxi and away I went.

Earlier that day I had phoned Paul Baker and asked him if he fancied a few beers later in the day unsurprisingly he responded by saying "sure thing, what time?" "Make it just after six" I told him, "Fine" he said and that was all there was to the beginning of my latest escape.

Just after six pm I sauntered into the pub we had agreed to meet in and was not surprised to find Paul already there sitting at a table with two pints of lager in front of him one was his and one was mine and the rest as they say is history.

Well not history exactly more of a mystery like many of the nights out I had in those days. I woke up the following morning on Paul's couch a bit worse for wear had a bite of breakfast said my goodbyes to Paul (who was also feeling a bit under the weather) and headed up the road to my own house to wait for a lift back to the hospital. When I say lift I mean of course I would wait until the police came for me.

When I got back to my house I did my usual went to the kitchen put on the kettle, popped into the living room and turned on the television went back to the kitchen waited for the kettle to boil, made a cup of tea grabbed a few biscuits and went back to living room to watch some TV. As it happened being in the middle of summer there was test match cricket on and England were playing the West Indies Now the one thing that people have never understood about me is why I a Scotsman could not only like cricket but also support England at cricket. (Not such a stereotypical Scot now am I?)

Well anyway I settled down to watch the cricket and was really getting into the game when ding-dong the doorbell went. I looked through the curtains and there they were PC Plod come to take me back to the hospital. Now I don't know what police are like where your from nut in Manchester they seem to have a protocol when dealing with mental health and that is two officers, one who is generally huge and does not say a lot, whilst the other tends to be much smaller and is the talker. I always thought it was a weird combination until I realized that the huge one was there purely for intimidation purposes and probably couldn't put two sentences together never mind properly caution anyone.

Anyway back to the story I went to the door an on opening it, said, "hello officers how can I help you?" We are looking for Ronald Coleman" the little cop spoke in a surprisingly soft voice. "Ron is in hospital" I replied "Can I help"? The little cop looked up at me and said " He has escaped from the hospital and is on a section of the mental health act so we are trying to find him" "Oh not again" I retorted he is always doing that" at this point I looked little cop straight in the eye and said, "well he is not here I'm sorry to say."   "Can we come in and have quick look?" little cop asked very politely I hasten to add. "Of course you can" I replied, "My name is Dave and I am one of the guys that shares the house with Ron" short pause "come on in" I showed them around the house including an empty bedroom telling them "this is Ron's room as you can see all of his stuff has been moved into storage while he is in hospital. Eventually we ended up in the living room where the little cop looked at the TV and said knowingly " you like cricket then?" A proper bright spark this one I thought to myself "Yes I do what about your self?" I replied, "Love it! I could watch it all day he said. Well in for a penny in for a pound I thought to myself before saying "Would you like a cup of tea or coffee"? The little one immediately said "tea thank you" The huge cop just grunted and shook his head in a motion that could only mean no. I went through to the kitchen and made the tea put a few biscuits on a plate and took it all back into the living room.

Strangely the big cop did not even sit down whilst the little cop and I drank our teas and watched the cricket. Twenty minutes later tea finished and the cricket just minutes from the lunch break little cop got to his feet and said " I guess we better be going then" with that he walked out of the living room with big cop close on his heals. I stepped in front of them to open the door saying " if Ron shows up here I'll call you at the station will I? "Yes you do that and thanks for the cup of tea" "no problem I replied. Even big cop sort of grunted something at this point, which I took as some kind of farewell grunt. "Bye" I called speaking to their retreating backs, then, swiftly I closed the door and started laughing.

After about ten minutes I once again regained a bit of self control and settled back to watch the lunch break interviews followed I hoped by a good afternoon of cricket. Some forty-five minutes into the afternoon session of play the doorbell went I looked out of the window and they were back, little cop and big cop were standing at the front door looking really pissed off. Slowly I went to the front door opened it and before I could say a word little cop exclaimed in a no nonsense voice "we know you're Ron Coleman. I looked at him and in a sarcastic voice retorted, "You will make detective one day mate".

Back to hospital for me then.

7 The psychiatrist' the plant and the windowsill

The inspiration for the title of this story comes from the lion the witch and the wardrobe by CS Lewis. The story itself was told to me by John Williams who heard it during one of his stays in hospital.

The story is set in Salford, England and is about a man who had started his psychiatric career diagnosed with drug-induced psychosis and then like many others progressed onto schizophrenia. The man lets call him John had been in services around eight years and was once again getting ready for discharge. This discharge was he decided going to be his last, he was determined to take a grip of his life and not come back to hospital.

John was called into his last ward round and came in ready to argue his case for discharge. He sat down made him self comfortable and looked the psychiatrist directly in the eye and said '' hello doc how are you today?" "I'm fine John what about you?" "I am really great" replied John I'm ready to go home stay home and get on with my life" The conversation continued for the next forty-five minutes the end result being John was told he would be discharged the

34

following day and would be sent an outpatient appointment.

For the next six months John turned up to his outpatient clinic and his life went on an upward track that so impressed his psychiatrist announced to him at the end of his sixth appointment " you know John I have been thinking that perhaps I will discharge you completely from services at our next appointment, Your life is now totally different from where it was". "You have a job, a social life, you're maintaining your flat well, your in a relationship I can see no need for us keeping you in services so think about it and if you agree we will discharge you from services. John nodded his assent and said "thank you" and went on his way.

The following month went by without incident and John showed up for his very last outpatient appointment armed with a pot plant as a gift for his psychiatrist. He placed the plant at the side of his chair sat down and once again told the psychiatrist how well things were going and again thanked him for all his help over the last few years. The psychiatrist told John that over the last year he (John) had shown amazing progress, that he had been a joy to work with and that the team had no doubts at all about discharging him from services. They both stood up and John shook hands with his psychiatrist both for the first and for the last time. John turned to walk out the room when he suddenly stopped, turned around, bent down picked up the plant and said to his now ex psychiatrist " I know it is not usual, but it came to me this morning that I wanted to mark this day in a special way by giving you this plant as a way of reminding you how I've grown in the last while and I hope you will accept this small token of my appreciation." The psychiatrist with a big grin on his face thanked John who promptly turned around walked out the door saying " bye-bye I'll not be back".

At the end of his out patient appointments the psychiatrist picked up the plant and gently placed it on the windowsill of his office. The next day he arrived in the office carrying a plant potholder into which he carefully placed his plant.

Over the next few months the psychiatrist lovingly cared for the plant but despite his tender ministrations he would often find that the plant was losing leaves without any apparent reason but he persisted it would appear to be getting better then the leaves would go again. There appeared to be no answer to this puzzle until one day a friend of the psychiatrist came to his office for a meeting to discuss the increasing numbers of people being admitted with drug induced psychosis.

The psychiatrist poured both of them coffee offered his friend a biscuit which was politely refused and was then astonished by his friends opening remarks, "okay Graham you can talk to me how long have you been smoking weed for?" "What do you mean how long have I been smoking weed for? I've never touched it in my life Bill"

"Come on Graham we are not all as stupid as we look what is it man? The stress of work perhaps or have you and Maggie been going through a difficult patch? You do know I will do anything I can to help you through this" "Help me through what Bill I haven't a clue what you are talking about, I have never used any drugs in my life, what makes you think I have started now for Gods; sake".

"Look behind you Graham the evidence is there that bloody great cannabis plant in your window sill" Graham looked behind him and then back at Bill his face now ashen white as he realized that the plant that John had given him was cannabis, he (Graham) was after all the regional lead for drug and alcohol services.

Nuff said.

8   The Conference (Adapted)

Billy Connelly is one of my favorite observational comedians and it is to him that this little story owes its birth. I have changed much of his story to suit psychiatry and though the story is not a true one the sentiment behind the story most certainly is.

Mental health conferences can be strange affairs, now a days, in this era of enlightenment most conferences follow a pattern you have professionals speaking, you have family members speaking and you have service users speaking, The professionals speak about their knowledge, the family members speak about their anguish and the service users speak about their experience. Many conferences are consensual in that people tend to be polite, this story all of it untrue is set prior to these days. It is set in Scotland at a time when there was a drive towards fifty/fifty conferences that is fifty percent of the audience were professionals and the other fifty percent were service users. It is also at a time when there was a war going on between professionals and service users, now to the story.

The time had arrived for the annual 50/50 conference in Scotland, and like all of these conferences in the past young Jimmy was

38

getting ready for the day ahead. Jimmy set off for the conference got on the bus to central Glasgow well ready for the day ahead. As the bus traveled into Glasgow Jimmy yawned and slowly but surely he fell asleep. Jimmy and sleep went together like cheese and wine and once asleep nothing would wake him so on he slept past the venue of the conference past the centre of the city and on to the bus terminus.

The bus driver had to wake Jimmy up and Jimmy realized he was now late for the start of the conference. He caught the next bus back to the conference centre rushed up the stairs and into the conference hall and quickly sat down.

After a few minutes Jimmy realized he had made a mistake and that he was sitting amongst the professionals worse than that he was now sitting in between two professionals who by their demeanor had noticed him and were obviously not happy at sitting beside a service user. As speaker after speaker spoke Jimmy could not contain himself he applauded when service users spoke and shook his head when professionals spoke. About half an hour into the session which was a panel session the professional to his left spoke to him saying "go get me a cup of coffee" seeing an opportunity to get out of where he was sat

Jimmy replied "no problem" and started to get up when the worker said "wait a minute leave your bag and give me one of your shoes, I just want to make sure you come back". Despondently Jimmy went off to get the coffee and some ten minutes later he returned with the coffee saying "queue" he handed the coffee over and was rewarded with the return of his shoe.

He took the shoe and there sitting right in the middle of the shoe looking back at him was a dollop of shit "put it on" the professional said Jimmy put his shoe back on. Jimmy sat there stoically determined to show no emotion then the other worker said, "go and get me a coffee and give me your other shoe". Once again Jimmy went on his way to get the coffee and again returned about ten minutes later coffee in hand. Giving the coffee to the professional he was handed back his other shoe, once again sitting in the middle of the shoe was a dollop of shit. "Put it on" the worker said. Jimmy complied pulling the shoe on aware that these two were going all out to humiliate him.

All through the session Jimmy maintained his composure and sat not saying a word. Just before lunch they called the last speaker of the morning and to the workers surprise it was Jimmy who was called to speak. He walked proudly to the podium in shoes full of shit, settled himself, looked at the audience, raised his hands to the heavens and said "colleagues in my humble opinion there will always be enmity between professionals and service users as long as they keep shitting in our shoes; and we comrades keep pissing in their coffees.

9   leave your libido at the door

Sex is a big taboo in psychiatry unless of course you are getting psychotherapy where it sometimes seems to us big Scottish males that if you are young pretty and female you have a good chance of getting psychotherapy normally from an old seedy male psychiatrist but if you're the aforementioned Scottish male then you have your psychotherapy through the point of a needle right into your bum.

Call me paranoid but this seems to be the experience of many of us though no doubt the answer we would get is that psychosis and talking therapies are contra-indicated. Of course un-be-knowing to the hospital staff Consumers even those not allowed too leave either the grounds or in these more modern times the ward have found the ways to ensure that our libidos are not left out of the game.

In the lets make love game in psychiatry timing is all important this for me was a really difficult concept for a start I thought until relatively recently that the Rhythm method was in actual fact the ability to make love to the beat of no woman no cry by Bob Marley and was totally gob smacked to discover that it was in actual fact a form of contraception allowed within the Roman Catholic faith.

42

But I digress and I want to tell you one of the big secrets left in Psychiatry today, the answer to how do we manage to have sex whilst being an inpatient question? What with all the staff round the ward, and the ensuing lack of any privacy what chance does one have of making love in the afternoon?

The answer is simple really the system suffers from a number of shortcomings one of these is that it actually believes its own propaganda so staff think that they always know what is happening with "their patients" in "their wards" during "their shifts" Well I can only say one thing in reply to "their thinking" and that is that this is "their delusion" and it happens on "their watch"

I am old enough to remember the big old psychiatric hospitals and in those days it was relatively easy to have a relationship well during the summer at least. People made love outside. When they moved all of psyche services into ordinary hospitals life got a bit more difficult for those who were in relationships. Necessity is however the mother of invention and it did not take us long to figure out how to get around this problem.

What we would do was simply wait until the afternoon handover; you see it was at this time of day when all the staff bar one (normally a young student nurse) would have a meeting that would regularly last forty-five minutes or more. As soon as the staff left for the meeting it was off we went to our bedrooms sometimes not alone. I often wondered what the student nurse thought as one by one or perhaps I should say two by two we left her alone.

So it was as simple as that, though it did not always go as planned. There was one occasion when having retired to my room with a visitor. Now I had been taught to always knock on a door before entering a room especially a bedroom. This does not seem to be true of our hospital based nursing staff who granted knock first but then just walk straight in without waiting for an answer.

So there I was in my room making love with a friend with not a care in the world appreciating the real value of the handover meeting when it happened a quick tap on the door of my room followed by a nurse crashing through the door.

She looked at me I looked at her my friend looked at her then at me we all looked at each other. The nurse was spluttering and coughing trying to get her words out. Finally she composed herself looked me straight in the eyes and in a loud voice said, "What do you think you're doing?" I just lay there in astonishment with my thoughts racing "what am I doing" I thought, I looked at the nurse and finally replied "Three years studying biology and you ask me what I am Doing".

What is our education system coming too.

10 Taking Nurses for a walk

I spent a lot of time on wards being what is called under special observations. This is where you have either one or two nurses with you twenty-fours a day no matter where you are. When you go to bed they are there, when you wake up they are there, when you have a shower or a bath they are there. The longest period I was specialed was for six weeks. Often when I am running training I ask participants what they think the worse thing about being specialed is?

It is amazing the answers you get they include, never being alone, no privacy, always feeling watched, not being able to have a bath or shower on your own. My favorite is when people say it must be going to the toilet to which I always reply "no that's revenge ".

I then go on to tell them that the worst thing about having two nurses with you twenty-four hours a day seven days a week is you can't masturbate. It is my honest and humble opinion that masturbation is not a spectator sport but is something that is better done in private. So as you can see being specialed was not my favorite state of being.

One of my biggest hates though was when you had to be escorted off the ward to go to the shops (normally to go for cigarettes) again I would have two nurses with me who would walk either side of me acting in a way that made it clear to anyone who saw us that I was being escorted.

There was on particular time I was being specialed by two nurses, I was sitting in a chair and they were sitting one on each side within touching distance of me. As usual I was being ignored by the two nurses who were engrossed in some heavy conversation about the staff night out the weekend just past. I felt like I was watching a game of tennis as they volleyed and lobbed chitchat and gossip about what had gone down over the weekend.

Finally after listening to this for about half an hour I had had enough, so I got out of my chair and started to walk across the room. Dutifully and in unison the nurses got out of their chairs and followed me across the room like a pair of faithful dogs always within touching distance. On reaching the other side of the room I sat down again but as soon as the nurses' bums touched their chairs I was up again and walking back to the other side of the room closely followed by my intrepid duo of nurses then on reaching the chairs sat again and waited for the one second break before the two nurses sat which was of course the signal for me to get up once again. Back and forward, back and forward I would go all day long never stopping not even realizing that the staff who were following me were constantly changing every forty five minutes or so thinking to myself that I was really pissing the staff off. Whilst they were merely writing in my notes

*Ron is really agitated today perhaps he needs more medication"

11 The Courtyard

The following story was told to me by a guy from Liverpool he swears it is true, I am not convinced but regardless of that it is a brilliant tale that deserves mention in this collection. For myself having spent a lot of time in locked units the highlight of the day was going out into the courtyard, where you could get fresh air (even though I spent most of my time smoking in the courtyard) and feel almost as if you were not stuck in some psychiatric unit. So the very fact the story is based on events in one of these courtyards makes it very easy for me to visualize this story.

There was a young woman (we will call her Jane) who had spent over six months in a locked ward never being allowed out, not even into the courtyard. During this time the closest thing to a friend that she had was a German Shepherd dog called dribble on account of the number of times a day the dog would go outside to do the toilet. Dribble was a patting dog and as the months dragged on they became inseparable so it came as no surprise that when Jane was finally allowed out into the courtyard that dribble would go with her. Jane started to look after dribble including cleaning up after Dribble, this mainly consisted of lifting the never-ending supply of pooh that dribble seemed to generate.

Over the next three months Jane continually asked if she could go out of the unit for a walk in the grounds of the hospital only to be told she was not ready. As time dragged on Jane got more and more frustrated until the day came when she finally blew up. In the past when this had happened she had really lost it and gotten angry then acted out in a way that meant she was injected and put in isolation then she would have to start all over again. This time she determined it would be different. Firstly, she contained her anger though she made sure that staff knew she was not happy with the situation. Then she implemented her plan she decided to go on a protest but one that could not be construed as part of her illness.

The day of the protest arrived and Jane followed as ever by Dribble went into the courtyard over the next hour Jane cleaned up the courtyard picking up all the pooh she could find. When she was done, instead of putting the bag of pooh she had collected into the bin provided she sat in the middle of the courtyard put on another pair of latex gloves emptied the pooh onto the grass beside her and started sculpting a figure from the dog shit.

She had been doing this for about 15 minutes when a nurse appeared in the courtyard came up to her and said "what do you think you are doing Jane" "I am sculpting" Jane replied. "So what are you sculpting"? the nurse asked. "Why its' you" Jane replied a wicked smile on her face. At this the nurse turned round and strode back to the hospital. Ten minutes after this the unit psychologist came into the courtyard walked up to Jane and without any pause said "okay Jane what are you doing"? "Why I am making a sculpture Dave" she replied "and what are you sculpting" Dave asked "Oh Dave, can't you see; its' you" Jane said. Dave mumbled something to himself then stomped out of the courtyard back into the unit.

Jane continued to model the dog shit for the next half hour stopping only to go and collect Dribbles next contribution to the sculpture. Jane had by now attracted a small group of admirers (and non-admirers) who were watching her sculpture of shit take shape. They were also waiting to see how events would unfold when the unit psychiatrist finally showed up. Out of nowhere he walked into the courtyard the consultant, you could tell he was the consultant because he wore a suit and walked in a way that said I am special. He surveyed the situation in an aloof

51

fashion peered at Jane then in his most doctor-ish voice said "Well Jane I know what you're doing" "what's that then doctor" Jane replied "why; you are making a model" said the consultant "that's right doctor" retorted Jane "And I know what it is Jane" "What's that then Doc" "It's a model of me isn't it Jane" at this there was a short pause then Jane stood up looked at the Doctor then looked at her sculpture of shit then back at the Doctor then said "Of course it is not a model of you stupid man I don't have enough shit"

12 DSM is it printed by Marvel comics? because it is funny

The Diagnostic Statistical Manual (DSM) is often referred to as the psychiatrists' bible as it is the book they use to diagnose people with mental illnesses. I have been fascinated by the DSM ever since I first discovered it existed, it should come as no surprise that it is not a book that I have found much in that I have agreed with. It is however a great source of material for humor and with every new bigger edition (we are now on DSMV) it seems to get ever more ridiculous, this for me means even more material.

Before I tell the story I want to tell you about a great party game that you can play with the DSM. What you do is when people arrive at the party you get them to open the DSM randomly and what ever page they open it they have to take on the characteristics associated with that diagnoses. The last time I played this I had to be anorexic bear in mind that at the time I weighed in at nearly 130Kgs.

As you might have guessed by now I have aspirations to be a stand up comedian, so the DSM is an important source book for me. Lets start by exploring some of the interesting diagnoses that you find in the DSM.

Spiritual Disorder is one of my favorite illnesses in the DSM, essentially what it tells us is that it is okay to talk to God that is called prayer but if God talks back to you: you are stuffed. In other words psychiatry is saying God is dead long live psychiatry. This denies one of the great beliefs that the three major religions Judaism, Christianity and Islam all hold to be true and that is that God is the same yesterday, today and tomorrow. So if god talked to the prophets yesterday then God must be talking to people today even though psychiatry begs to differ.

More and more areas of our lives are now being controlled by psychiatry, one of the best examples of this is social phobia disorder this sounds like a serious thing to have but it only became a disorder after they discovered that Ritalin could make shy people more confident. So some of the symptoms of social phobia disorder are blushing in social situations, an inability to maintain eye contact in social situations and using alcohol or other substances as a crutch to manage social situations. This serious illness is treated by the aforementioned drug an amphetamine based substance; only thing new here is we have a legitimate dealer.

In DSM IV there is an illness called hypersexual activity disorder, now this is an illness that I do want but can I get it not in anybody's lifetime why? Well funnily enough it is an illness that only women can get. Lets get this straight this biological condition only affects the minds of women get a life.

Why do I call the DSM a Marvel comic publication because I marvel at the contents and laugh at the rationale and some of the stuff they come up with in DSM would not be out of place in a Marvel comic superhero story? Anyway if the DSM was a serious medical publication then why are so many of them sold to Insurance companies?

As I finish this chapter I am ready for a coffee oops or should I say I am about to indulge in one of my Caffeine related disorders (DSM IIIR)

Now there's a thing

13 Victor and the mobile phone

The following story has in the past been described as an urban myth has been told by different people and has according to them been based in many different cities. As ever this story has its' roots firmly in reality and only the name of the individual at the heart of the story has been changed. I know that this is no myth why? Well it's simple really I was there as they say.

This story takes place in the City of Birmingham in the late 1990's during the time when community care was still a fairly new Government policy. It was also a time where everything that was done in psychiatry had to be called a therapy, where we all ran around shouting fidelity to the model, fidelity to the model and death to those who practiced infidelity to the model. Well I'm happy to say in those days I was an infidel and models meant nothing to me.

Anyway Mike Smith the director of nursing practice (my co-author on Working with Voices) collared me in a coffee shop one morning to have a chat. Always beware being bought a coffee by any senior management person as it always means more work and true to form he told me. There was a growing problem for many service users who were voice hearers and responded out loud to their voices in public places, and he wanted a solution that would stop this from happening.

At the next meeting of the team I was working with an assertive outreach team at the time we discussed this problem and spent a lot of time brain storming ideas, after an hour it was clear we were getting nowhere so we decided to have a break and go for a coffee. On the way to the coffee shop there was a man on a mobile phone having a massive argument with someone on the other end of the line. He was shouting fairly loudly and gesticulating wildly yet no one seemed bothered by this and people were passing him by as if it was the most normal thing in the world.

At that moment a new "therapy" was being born in my mind Cognitive Mobile Phone Behavioral Therapy. I called it this really to confuse our psychology department at this point in time were CBT crazy everything had CBT attached to it so in a moment of naughtiness I followed suit. I was able to picture in my head how it would work.

The way things were happening at the time was simple a person that was hearing voices and needed to respond to them would do so normally by talking out loud to them and other people would become concerned for the person often calling the police who would then bring the person to us. We would very quickly send the person back home then the Police would get called again the next time it happened and so the cycle of services continued to operate even when it was not required.

The plan was simple we would give all those who we knew spoke out loud to their voices a mobile phone. We even had a ready supply of mobiles lying around the services in cupboards and desk drawers. They were old mobiles no longer used none had sim cards and most no longer had batteries. We gathered the mobile phones together and went out and visited the clients we knew would benefit from having a mobile phone and talked to them about how they could use it when they felt the need to respond to their voices.

We suggested that when they had to talk back they should take the phone out of their pocket press any number and then talk freely to their voices. This would then appear perfectly normal to all those who were around and no one would contact the police allowing the voice hearer to get on with their life.

We had one voice hearer in particular who used this strategy his name was Victor and he had terrible voices a lot of the time especially when he was using public transport. During every journey Victor would be on his "mobile phone" from start to finish talking to his voices telling them to back off or shut up but as soon as the journey was over he would "hang up" and get on with what he was doing.

Victor has become a legend in his own lifetime because of what happened one-day in December. As many people involved in psychiatric services know December is a strange month in the psychiatric calendar. It is the month of the year when many teams organize trips out to places where shopping is the main thing on the itinerary and our team was no different from any other and this particular year we decide to have a trip to London.

Now part of a team trip out involves convincing enough clients to go with you to justify the trip, when I was a client the convincing factors for me was that the trip would cost nothing, the food was free and that there would be the opportunity for a beer or two also free. Thankfully clients had not changed much in this respect so through gentle bribery we got the required numbers so the trip to London to do our Christmas shopping was on. One of the clients going with us was of course Victor. Finally the day of travel arrived and we found ourselves standing on the platform at Birmingham New Street station waiting for our train.

Victor boarded the train and sat opposite me in a four-seated area with a table between us. Victor was his usual self in that as soon as the train started out came the mobile and Victor very quickly was talking with his voices, him sounding very much like someone with a lot to discuss.

The Journey was uneventful as Victor kept up a constant narrative on his phone. Then came that moment when we entered a long tunnel you know the moment, you're in the middle of a phone call and the phone signal goes on every ones' phone who is on the train; except Victors, he keeps his conversation going with no interruption all the way into the London station. Once the train has stopped at the station Victor presses a button on his mobile and puts in his pocket. At that moment a guy in a suit comes over to where we are all getting our stuff together taps Victor on the shoulder and when Victor turns around says in a posh voice "excuse me can you tell me what kind of mobile phone that is?" Victor looked at the man and within a blink of eye relied "it's a new satellite version now fuck off"

Honest, it is the truth I was there.

60

14 Christmas in the psychiatric unit

Schizophrenic Christmas Carol:
Do you Hear What I Hear?

The following piece has been delivered by myself for a number of years now and is made up of a number of Christmas's that I spent in psychiatric hospitals detained under the mental health act. I have purposefully merged them all into one day in order to explore how such a significant day in the Christian calendar can be trivialized by the psychiatric system. It is also important to understand that Christmas in this story does not last one day but is much more a period of time that starts about week before Christmas and ends around the 3rd or 4th of January.

It has always amazed me how around the 21st to the 24th of December previously seriously "mentally ill" people have these miraculous recoveries' and are allowed home before the festive season starts. I have sat there watching them as they leave broad smiles on their faces waving at me and saying things like "merry Xmas" or "have a good time Ron "fuck off" was my reply to the words of salutation from my former fellow inmates.

I have also watched them return in early January smiles gone, heads bowed, unable to speak and looks that peer through you from eyes that have no spark I do not know what happens between the last two weeks of December and the end of that first week in January but the one thing I do know is I don't want to know.

So there I am in the ward most people on leave so all is quiet. I am enjoying watching sport and movies and am looking forward to watching boxing-day test cricket which is Australia versus England but that is still two days away and before it I have to go through the nightmare that is Christmas day in the psychiatric unit.

It all kicks off early on Christmas morning starting from when the early shift of ward staff arrives. Imagine the scene it is an acute psychiatric ward the few patients left in the ward are not being allowed home for Christmas in other words those left are regarded as the most distressed and vulnerable patients in the hospital and I am one of them.

Once the staff arrives it begins, the staff troop into the ward where we are sitting they are all wearing these really strange hats that have tentacles coming from them that look to some like snakes and to others like some alien's features from Star Wars they then start calling happy Christmas to everyone in high pitched shrill voices whilst running about like a banshee at some weird Yuletide pagan ceremony. Remember they are doing this in an acute psychiatric ward with the most distressed of their clients. If I had worn a hat like that and went running around like a mad man screaming merry Christmas they would have sectioned me to the psych ward. The rest of the morning is spent calming down all those who freaked out at the strange Christmas welcome.

The next big thing I noticed that was different about Christmas and the other 364 days of the year in the unit was that there was an addition to the staff team who only appeared on Christmas day. If you watched the office carefully you would spot the ward manager sneaking out of the office for the first time in a year. You could tell it was the ward manager because of the paleness of his skin he had not seen sunlight in 364 days he had spent all of these days locked in his office doing this thing called the Rota. It was only after five years of being in the psychiatric system that I discovered that the Rota was not some kind of specialized clinical intervention that required a ward manager a room and lots of concentration.

Next on the Christmas list was the dreaded Christmas dinner. For the rest of the year we would meekly queue up for our meals get what we wanted then sit down eat and get out of the dinning room but no not on Christmas day. On this day alone we would walk into the dinning room to sit at tables that were decked out with cutlery, (plastic) napkins (paper) glasses (more plastic) and my worst nightmare Christmas crackers (more paper & more Plastic).

The staff then served us Christmas dinner at our seats with the refrain "enjoy you dinner", the reply is normally "thanks". Finally it is my turn "enjoy your Christmas dinner Ron, pull your cracker and put your Christmas hat on" The nurse says "fuck off" is my reply.

Anyway after the agony of dinner and an afternoon snooze we are all herded together back to the main lounge to play games. Now if you have ever worked in a psychiatric unit or been a psychiatric patient you will know that between workers and patients there are no such things as games it is war. For service users it is the only time we can beat the staff and there is nothing they can do about it, as a consequence of this we tend to take games really, really seriously.

After the dinner we were given our presents as usual it was a pair of socks and some after-shave that was probably mass-produced in someone's shed it was the same stuff every year I called it Ode de piss because of its smell. We were then given one can of beer the height of our Christmas celebration was this one can of beer and every year they made the same mistake and gave a can to the recovering alcoholic who would run around the unit trying to finish it off whilst being chased by staff trying to get it off him he would be shouting at them "no you can't have it back its mine, its mine you gave it to me; my precious" This scene would be our entertainment for the next hour or so and then it would be all quiet on the western front so to speak.

There we were then on Christmas evening sitting in the lounge playing trivial pursuit on one side there was me and another patient and on the other side was two staff nurses. The game was intense until finally me and the other guy had collected six cheeses and answered the question in the middle and lo it came to pass (well it is Christmas) that we won. After a quick lap of honor around the table and a celebratory hug we sat back down to enjoy that feeling that comes with victory I call it smugness.

One of the staff nurses went off without a word no doubt to fester and lick their wounds. The other one sucked it up and came over to congratulate us she put her hand on my shoulder and said "Well done Ron you answered a lot of really obscure questions in that game I don't know how you did it." I looked around the room to make sure no one could hear me apart from the nurse and said:

"Well it was really easy Jane you see I have seven other voices to confer with"

15 Shorts

Psychiatrist: So what's your problem? Patient: I prefer patterned socks to plain socks. Psychiatrist: There's nothing wrong with that. Lots of people prefer patterned socks to plain socks. I do myself. Patient: So how do you like yours - fried or boiled?

A man who thinks he's George Washington has been seeing a psychiatrist. He finishes up one session by telling him, "tomorrow, we'll cross the Delaware and surprise them when they least expect it." As soon as he's gone, the psychiatrist picks up the phone and says, "King George, this is Benedict Arnold. I have the plans."

Three psychiatrists are talking about how everyone comes to them with their problems but they have no one to go to with their problems. They agree to share their problems with each other.
The first psychiatrist says, "I'm addicted to Barbiturates. I write myself prescriptions all the time."
The second psychiatrist says, "I'm a compulsive gambler. I overcharge my patients to pay for my gambling addiction."
The third psychiatrist says, "I can't keep a secret. My patients tell me their secrets in confidence and I divulge it to everyone."

When Tom and Charles were on their daily walk, the passed a restaurant and decided to get something to eat.

"Tom!" exclaimed Charles. "We can't go in, Can't you see the sign 'NO PETS ALLOWED'." Oh, I see it," replied Tom. "That doesn't matter."

He puts his sunglasses on and walks up to the door, but before he could take another step, the doorman stops him and says, "I'm sorry sir, no pets allowed in this restaurant." "Look Mr.," Tom responds loudly "I'm blind, this is my seeing-eye dog!" "Since when is a German Shepherd a seeing-eye dog?" the doorman responded. "It's the latest kind of seeing-eye dog, how could you not know?" Tom shouted.

Seeing Toms' success, Charles tried walking in with his Poodle. Before he even said a word, the doorman stopped him, "don't tell me that a Poodle is the latest type of seeing-eye dog!"

Thinking as fast as he could, Charles quickly answered back in an upset voice.

"You mean to tell me that they gave me a Poodle?"

The psychiatrist moves close to the young man in the hospital room. He is staring

68

straight ahead oblivious to his surroundings. Suddenly he starts yelling, "I can't see! I can't see!"

Taken aback, the psychiatrist turns to the boy's mother who is sitting nearby, "Has long has this been going on?"

"Ever since you stepped in front of the TV Doctor." was the Mothers response.

16 The Schizophrenic Rat and Other Tall Tales

It is a terrible thing when science is used to promote ideas that have very little or no scientific validity. Yet all the time we are told the schizophrenia is a real biological illness that must be controlled by medication. Yet nothing can be further from the truth there is no scientific evidence that this is the case, instead the real evidence is hidden behind many dubious ideas and theories about schizophrenia.

One of my favorites is the following story scientists' have given rats schizophrenia by giving them injections and then treated them with anti-psychotics. Wow wait a minute was my immediate thought to this claim. How do we know the rats in question had schizophrenia? Is Dr Doolittle actually a psychiatrist as well as a vet? Did Doolittle carry out a psychiatric state evaluation? Of course not, so how could this kind of claim be evidenced. As I thought about this the image of a young Doctor in a white coat came into my head the doctor walked up to a cage wherein was said schizophrenic rat and addressing the rat said "Tell me Rolland do you hear you voices inside your head or outside your head squeak once for inside your head and twice for outside your head" on hearing Rolland rat respond by squeaking twice the young doctor says "well that confirms it you have a serious metal illness call schizophrenia and we shall start treatment immediately."

LSD was also given to research subjects in an attempt to create schizophrenia in humans I tried really hard to sign up for that research.

But Beat this one

Now comes the surprising finding by a German research team that chlamydia may be linked with schizophrenia. Dr Rudolf Wank, an immunologist at the Ludwig-Maximilians-University in Munich, has reported recently that schizophrenic patients are much more likely to be infected with one or more variants of chlamydia. More importantly, he found that targeting the bug with specially treated immune cells improved the patients' symptoms dramatically.

About 40 per cent of the 75 patients he studied were infected with chlamydia, compared with 6 per cent in the control group (ie, people who did not have schizophrenia). As Dr Wank explains: "Chlamydia comes in three varieties, two of which can cause a flu-like respiratory infection or pneumonia, while the third causes the sexually transmitted disease.

The patients were much more likely to have one or more of these." The team also found that the risk of developing schizophrenia rose dramatically for patients with a certain group of immune system genes. My view is simple this is the research that coined the phrase What A Wanker.

Cats Cause Schizophrenia
The infectious agent that currently stands the best chance of being indicted as a cause of schizophrenia is Toxoplasma gondii, a protozoan parasite. Its definitive host is the cat, which is unaffected by the parasite. Humans become infected by inhaling or ingesting the cysts from cat feces from a litter box, garden, sandbox or children's play area. You can also get infected by drinking contaminated water or by eating undercooked meat from a lamb, pig or other animal that has become infected. In the U.S. 10% to 25% of people are infected. Transmission of T. gondii to the fetus of pregnant women is known to produce dire consequences for the developing brain such as mental retardation and retinal problems. Transmission to children or adults has been assumed to have no serious consequences, but that is now being reconsidered.
The linkage to schizophrenia is intriguing. Individuals who are infected have almost a threefold chance of having schizophrenia

compared with those not infected. Two studies reported that the offspring of women who have antibodies to T. gondii at birth are more likely to develop schizophrenia when they grow up. And two other studies found that people with schizophrenia have had more exposure to cats in childhood compared with individuals who do not have schizophrenia. Other studies have shown that T. gondii can change the personality traits of humans who are infected.

Many drugs used to treat schizophrenia also suppress Toxoplasma in cell culture. That opens the possibility, now being studied, of using additional anti-T. gondii drugs to treat schizophrenia. Someday a vaccine might prevent schizophrenia.

Many questions remain unanswered, especially why so many people are infected but so few develop schizophrenia. Nothing has been definitively proven, and no infectious agent has been convicted. So don't get rid of your cat yet.

17 The Things They Said.
"The reason I talk to myself is because I'm the only one whose answers I accept."
— George Carlin

"I became insane, with long intervals of horrible sanity."
— Edgar Allan Poe

"It is sometimes an appropriate response to reality to go insane."
— Philip K. Dick, VALIS

"Mad Hatter: "Why is a raven like a writing-desk?"
"Have you guessed the riddle yet?" the Hatter said, turning to Alice again.
"No, I give it up," Alice replied: "What's the answer?"
"I haven't the slightest idea," said the Hatter"
— Lewis Carroll, Alice in Wonderland

"We do not have to visit a madhouse to find disordered minds; our planet is the mental institution of the universe." Johann Wolfgang von Goethe

"People can do great things. However, there are some things they just CAN'T do. I, for instance, have not been able to transform myself into a Popsicle, despite years of effort."

— Brandon Sanderson, Alcatraz Versus the Evil Librarians

"Perhaps if you know you are insane then you are not insane. Or you are becoming sane, finally." Philip K. Dick

"One must be sane to think clearly, but one can think deeply and be quite insane." Nikola Tesla

18 To John Williams ("After you speak in a group, listen to hear if you said anything.")

This chapter is dedicated to John Williams who sadly died a number of years ago from a sudden heart attack. John was a stalwart of the hearing voices office in Manchester. John was a really funny guy who told jokes all the time and had an amazing laugh that could cheer up anyone. The following are the kind of stories and jokes I know he would enjoy.

A Concise History Of Psychiatry.

2000 B.C. - Here, eat this root.

1000 A.D. - That root is heathen. Here, Say this prayer.

1850 A.D. - That prayer is superstition. Here, drink this potion.

1940 A.D. - That potion is snake oil. Here, swallow this pill.

1985 A.D. - That pill is ineffective. Here, take this new pill

2000 A.D. - That new pill is not working. Here, eat this root.

Welcome to the psychiatric helpline.

Hello and welcome to the psychiatric helpline. Please listen carefully to the following choices as our menu has recently changed.

If you are obsessive-compulsive, please press 1 repeatedly.

If you are co-dependent, please ask someone else to press 2.

If you have multiple personalities, please press 3, 4, 5 and 6.

If you are paranoid-delusional, we know who you are and what you want, stay on the line and we will get to you.

If you are schizophrenic, listen carefully and a little voice will tell you which number to press.

If you are manic-depressive, it doesn't matter which number you press. No one will answer.

A series of one-liners

"Reality can be hell when you're only visiting."

"We're all here because we're not all here."

"Ten out of ten people die-so-don't take life too seriously."

"Constructive criticism: I tell you what's wrong with me.

Destructive criticism: You tell me what is wrong with me."

"Now I can wake up and say, "Good morning, God!" rather than "Good God, it's morning!"

Attitude Adjustment

A little rabbit is happily running through the forest when he stumbles upon a giraffe rolling a joint. The rabbit says, "Giraffe my friend, why do you do this?

Come with me running through the forest! You'll see, you'll feel so much better!" The giraffe looks at him, looks at the joint, tosses it and goes off running with the rabbit.

Then they come across an elephant snorting coke, so the rabbit again says, "Elephant my friend, why do you do this? Think about your health. Come running with us through the pretty forest! You'll see, you'll feel so good!" The elephant looks at them, looks at his razor, mirror and all, then tosses them and starts running with the rabbit and giraffe.

The three animals then come across a lion about to shoot up and the rabbit says, "Lion my friend, why do you do this? Think of what you are doing to your body! Come running with us through the sunny forest! You will feel so good!"

The lion puts down his needle, picks up the rabbit and starts beating him. As the giraffe and elephant watch in horror they say, "Lion, why did you do this? He was merely trying to help us all!"

The lion says, "He always makes me run around the forest for hours every time he's on ecstasy.

Reflection

The reason I talk to myself is because I'm the only one whose answers I accept.

During a visit to the mental asylum, Guy asked the Director what the criterion was that defined whether or not a patient should be institutionalized.

'Well,' said the Director, 'we fill up a bathtub, then we offer a teaspoon, a teacup, and a bucket to the patient and ask him or her to empty the bathtub.'

'Oh, I understand,' said Guy. 'A normal person would use the bucket because it's bigger than the spoon or teacup.

'No.' said the Director, 'A normal person would pull the plug. (Pause.)

... Guy, do you want a bed near the window?'

19 Diagnosing the Blues

I have written a lot about escaping from psychiatric units in this book and that is because every time I was locked up in one I thought about nothing else. I used to often tell myself it was my duty as a POW (prisoner on ward) to escape.

Most of my escapes tell a story of one kind or another but the following one I must admit I did for the sheer hell of it. My Psychiatrist at this time was in charge of psychotherapy for the whole of greater Manchester but being Schizophrenic as I was labeled denies one access to such niceties as talking therapies.

Over time I had got to know this psychiatrist I knew that he was a secret smoker, a dodgy dealer of Psychotropic pills and potions, and to cap it all he was a miserable maker of music within the blues tradition. Indeed my unfriendly Doctor worst kept secret was that he was the drummer in a band called Diagnosing the blues.

Well I mean you could not make this stuff up! Drummer! This I had to see for myself so I kept my ear to the ground and bided my time until I got the information I was looking for. My consultant psychiatrist was playing a gig not far from the hospital at the Manchester City Football Clubs social club. Brilliant I thought a night out was beckoning. I made my plans which involved me escaping from the unit heading over to the social club getting in and listening to his band all while remaining out of his sight until I was ready to say hello!

All went to plan I got out of the ward even though it was locked by attaching myself to visitors and just walking past the nurse (another agency nurse) who was in charge of the door. Paid to get into the social club, bought the guy who signed me in a pint and sat myself down with a beer and waited for the music to start.

When it started (they were actually not bad) I just sat and listened to the first three or four tracks they played. They had just launched into a Fleetwood Mac track called need your love so bad when I decided it was time for the little drummer boy to get sight of me. I stood up slowly and waited finally he looked straight at me did a double take and then he just stared at me and played his drums, stared and played, stared and played his facial color was changing through various hues of red and purple. As they went into the last verse of the song I made my way out of the club passing right beside the band giving him the finger and saying in a loud voice analyze that.

20 To Parents and other Inner Critics

A Poem to my Parents

You are right and I am wrong;
Why did it take me oh so long
to come upon this realization?
(must be my poor imagination)

Everything I say and do
could better have been done by you!
Bless me – I don't have your hindsight –
Of course, with that, how could you NOT be right?

A thing to do should not have been started
A thing to finish should've been left alone
Right should be left, and the left should be right!
To all these transgressions I admit to, and moan;
"How I wish I were as perfect
as your highest expectations…"
But alas it is my lot, I see,
to bear your constant lamentations
All that you know, and care to share
is SURELY for my own welfare!
I know this, but it's never enough,
never measures up, never up to snuff

In your ultimate wisdom, which you generously share,
from the tiniest ways I conduct my affairs,
to plans that run foul of where YOU think I should be,
I KNOW now it's hopeless for me just to be ME!

I've but two last wishes; that in your greatness,
your knowledge might only be matched with some patience,
and that you'd forgive me as I muddle along –
For you're always right – and I, always wrong…

G.P.
June, '96

21 More Shorts

The following are a collection of very short almost one-line stories and jokes I have either used or picked up from others over the years.

If you see a psychiatrist and you have a straight face and are hearing voices you're schizophrenic, if you see a psychiatrist and you are laughing and hearing voices you're manic and if the psychiatrist does not like you and you are hearing voices you have a personality disorder.

What do you get if you cross a psychiatrist with an actor? Answer: A doctor who not only thinks he is god but plays the part rather well.

I was speaking at a one-day event in Oxford a few years ago on schizophrenia when someone in the audience shouted to me "what is a burnt out schizophrenic then?" without thinking I responded "Joan of Arc"

My stepdaughter Alex told me the following one not long after being told she probably had Attention Deficit Hyperactivity Disorder (ADHD). How many people with ADHD does

85

it take to change a light bulb she asked? I don't know how many? I dutifully answered, "look behind you a bicycle." she then shouted.

Many years ago we would bare our souls to the priest when we had problems now we bare our bums to the community psychiatric nurse.

What do you call a psychiatrist with an erection? Answer a psychotherapist.

Why did the chicken cross the road?

Answer to get to the other side.

Why did the psychiatrist cross the road?

Answer to detain the chicken

What is the difference between God and a psychiatrist?

Answer God does not think he is a psychiatrist.

What about a sequel to Women are from Venus and Men are from Mars, called Women are from Venus, Men are from Mars and Psychiatrists are from Uranus.

22 The House Husband Journal

My Time as a House Husband

Well I'm 2 weeks into being the house husband and I love it (Karen told me to say that) being a man I cannot Multi-Task (Karen told me to say that as well) my two kids Rory and Francesca have decided that I need to learn the full extent to Karen's role when I am away and are doing nothing to help without the threat of losing income from me this works sometimes and at other times they do not seem to care.

They do not believe me when I tell them they are grounded for a year my daughter has already developed her mothers glare that just says hahaha no way.

The problem is they are right I could not bear to have them in the house for a year so groundings get down graded to final warnings all the time by me.

The second area I am having real difficulty with is of course meals I find that most evenings I am making three different meals I

make a suggestion and one will say yes and the other will say no as I try to work through this one will say can I have for dinner I say good idea the other says I hate that I say what would you like then they say I want -----
I say why do we not all have that The other says but I hate that more than I hate anything and any way you said what I want is good the other chimes in that you have just told me that I can have what I suggested.

Game set and match you have been doubled teamed by your knuckle dragging son and your wife- copying daughter. So you cook both then you realize that there is not enough for you Cheese and Toast Again Then.

Two weeks in 14 weeks to go well I'm in it to win it: more soon

House Husband update week 4

You may have noticed there was no post last week and there is a really simple reason for that it was half term. Francesca told me the day before it started it was simply said I told her it was bed time and she replied no dad off school for a week its half term, I thought she was kidding me half term lasts a week a week the scary daughter was going to be home all day every day for a week. I was now scared.

My son who turned 18 over the last few days also decided to get into the Spirit of half term (even though he is not at school) by announcing that he was supporting his sister by ensuring that she enjoyed half term by him staying in bed all day and not disturbing her. He is the son who thinks when I look him in the eye and tell him "get a Job' that this is me in his words "messing with his head"

To cut a long story short the two them had my running about after them like a blue arsed fly the scary one decided the instead of me being in charge of just the evening meal I was now in charge of all three meals and supper as well threatening to phone child-line citing neglect if I did not make the meals.

Once again Scary daughter got the better of me. I am going to start a campaign to ban half term personally I think its all teachers fault. Next time my son goes job- hunting Ha ha and Scary daughter takes me Internet shopping till then may all half terms be short

House Husband Update Week 5ish I think Part One:

There comes a point when time becomes meaningless to the house husband and it seems to me that I am getting there and once again who helped me realize this, was, yes you've guessed it Scary Daughter Francesca. Who informed me that she was having a sleep over last weekend just before I was inducted into on-line grocery shopping and that she (as my Trainer) would go on-line with me to pick what she wanted for that weekend.

At the mention of food something happened Rory (son who is Finding himself) appeared to say he would be going on-line before me also. After Francesca finished finding Festival food and Rory rampaged riotously round the keyboard with great gusto I systematically started shopping for what I wanted. I bought Milk, Eggs, Bacon and bread the pressed the button to the checkout.

Ping £176.78p appeared on the screen, The room started spinning my legs felt like jelly how could the shopping cost me that amount. Regaining control I named the problem loudly Francesca, Rory get yourselves down here now!

They both arrived beside me and stood just

behind me as I sat staring senselessly at the screen. "What's wrong with this" I said pointing to the screen Francesca looked at me like I was losing the plot and said in her little girlie voice only ever heard by me "I don't know daddy" to which Rory said in a superior voice "You're Stupid Frankie anyone can see the problem".

Rory then proceeded to lean over press something on the keyboard at which point the computer pinged again and those immortal words appeared "your purchase was successful" followed by "you have saved £13.00 by shopping with us and gained 176 Tesco points.

House Husband Update Week 5ish Part Two

At the end of part one I was slowly coming to terms with how much I had paid for the online food shopping Rory (he who is expensively finding himself using my wallet) informed me that he was looking forward to next weeks shop. Another Shop I screamed silently to myself refusing to let Rory see I was fazed by this comment.

The next day was Friday and as scary daughter had been telling me the whole week this was her birthday weekend sleepover with her best friend Wizbit.

I pointed out to scary daughter that people myself included had what we called a birthDAY not a Birthday Weekend the only exception I knew to this rule was the queen who also celebrated her birthday twice a year. Scary Daughter was having none of it from us peasants i.e. me as she informed me that she would be taking over the Lounge area as her and Wizbit, were going to watch every Harry Potter movie made.

Worst was to come I was not to enter the lounge upon the pain of death as they would also be practicing putting on their makeup and my role would be to be based in the kitchen and respond to their food requests.

I decided enough was enough and that I would not be ordered around by Scary Daughter, "Francesca Come here I need to talk to you now" I called with my angry voice on. "What is it Daddy" Scary daughter replied with her childish voice. This is the voice she uses when she thinks I am angry and I admit it I fall for it every time except this time I want to watch the football on Saturday and Sunday so you can't take over the Lounge. Okay daddy she said: looking at me with her most hurt look and pouty bottom lip.

One moment I had won the lounge back looking at her tear filled eyes instead of claiming this rare victory I heard myself say " well your only 14 once I guess you can have the lounge for one weekend". I looked around to see if someone else had spoken these words but no it was me, So scary daughter got her own way and I spent the weekend in Kitchen playing Butler.

As if that was not enough Rory (still finding himself) phoned on the Sunday to tell me he had got himself a job I must confess I thought I had lost the plot and that I was hearing things Rory a Job, Work, wages, no it could not be true. Later that day Karen confirmed my worst fears she phoned and told me Rory was starting work but I must have imagined it.

House Husbands update the final Chapter

I must confess this final entry in my house-husband adventure has taken me a bit of time to get right mainly because so much is happening at the moment. Firstly Karen is on her way home and has already made it clear during our last Skype call before she left Australia that all the changes I had made in the kitchen were to be reversed and it would once again be her domain. Personally I think she is being a bit precious about the kitchen, after all it has been me that has had to cook and use the kitchen over the last eight weeks so it should now be considered my domain.

I ran "its my kitchen" idea by scary daughter, her response was simple and went like this ha ha ha ha ha ha ha ha he he he he he he your dead dad. (At time of writing Karen arrived home the time it has taken me to recover and write this shows the outcome of Kitchen domain debate)

At the same time as scary daughter was laughing her head off at my feeble attempts of gaining control, my son Rory (still finding himself) gave a whole new meaning to earning a living. In the last diary entry I was slowly adjusting to the fact that Rory had got himself a job. When the day came for Rory to start work Guess who had to get up at six something in the morning to wake Rory up. Yes your right it was ME! I then had to make his breakfast ME! Coax him out of bed ME! Give him his bus fare ME! Then see him out the door ME! Come to think about the only thing I didn't do was go and do his days' work for him.

This drama has been repeated every single working day since and was only topped on the day that Rory received his first wage. I seem to remember when I was a youngster and got my first real job that paid proper wages that on receipt of my wages I would hand them all over to my mum who would give me my pocket money the rest would be for my keep. She would also give me bus fare every day plus my lunch box. I thought that this was fair and so expected Rory to do the same that is hand over his wage packet.

This more than anything else was to show me how naive I am and that the househusband life was not as idyllic as I thought it would be. Payday arrived Rory came home as usual, grunted at me as usual, he then went upstairs as usual.

So I made dinner as usual, shouted for them to come down for dinner as usual we ate dinner as usual and when dinner was over Rory got up to go back upstairs as usual. "Wait a minute Rory" I said have you not forgotten something. "Sorry dad" he said clearly thinking and a smile came to his face as he spoke again "thanks for Dinner dad"". He was about to head off upstairs again when out of my mouth the words finally came "did you get paid today" I asked. "Yes" he retorted "Well come on then hand it over" Rory looked genuinely perplexed as he said "Hand what over" "Your wage packet you silly numpty" I said now even more perplexed looking than Rory was.

To cut a long story short, Rory had no intention of handing over his Pay packet he even expected me to get him up everyday, make his breakfast and lunch box every day, to give him his bus fare every day and of much more importance to me to let him keep all of wages to himself. Indeed his first response when I suggested handing over his wage packet went as follows ha ha ha ha ha ha ha ha he he he he he Dad you're killing me.

I was determined not to let the kids have won every sparring contest we had over my short house husband career. So I waited till Karen came home thinking I would deploy her as my secret weapon and that she would relieve Rory of the burden of holding his own wages.

I bided my time and when we were all sitting down for dinner the day after Karen came back I mentioned the fact that Rory had now been paid but had handed not one penny over for his keep. I waited for the sparks to fly and Rory to get what for from Karen. Instead she turned to me and told me we now lived in the 21st Century and I was acting like some 18thCentury slum landlord and that our Son (who is still finding himself) needs to keep his money so he can explore who he is.

Karen then announced my house husband days were at an end and that the next part of my journey would be getting myself a new healthy lifestyle that would see me change diet use mindlessness I mean mindfulness and meditation I would become a neo vegetarian and cut out all the food groups that were bad for me Noooooooooooooooooo.

Keep up to date on how my new "lifestyle" is going by joining my face book Page.

23 Crofter's diary

I have been keeping a diary of life on the croft and wanted to share a day I had last year
August 12th 2010

Morning: Up to water and feed the 45pigs and two children don't know which is worse. Of the 45 pigs 29 are piglets the oldest piglets are 5 weeks today. There are 12 of them and they are full of fun and interact with me better than my kids do. It's sad to think that they (the piglets) will be leaving in the next couple of weeks. As I was feeding them I realized that though I will only have my piglets for six to eight weeks I have my kids for life. Amazing what you think about when your feeding pigs.

Its' not only the pigs and kids I have to feed and water this morning but also our chickens, geese, ducks, two cats and a dog and of course our paranoid, aggressive and often violent cockerel. He doesn't like me at all and I must confess the feeling is mutual.

Nearly every day he lies in wait to attack me

and today was no exception. I try to sneak into the pen but he was waiting yet again. There is a routine here he lets me into the pen and ignores me as I walk to the feeder and fill it he even lets me collect the three eggs that are there today. It is as I walk back to the gate that I see him standing there between me and the gate he looks at me then without warning he attacks. He jumps in the air his spur out to the front like some kind of deadly demented kung fu master.

This morning however I am prepared, I have padded up and am ready for him his spur hits my well protected leg and instead of the usual scream from me I stand and stare silently daring him to attack again, he looks at me just for a moment it's almost a thoughtful look before he turns away and saunters back to his harem of clucking chicks honor seemingly satisfied. I walk to the gate head held high, unhurt for once and in a moment of madness give myself a high five.

Afternoon
Finished the lunchtime feeds and just got ready to go into town where the annual international market is on. The two kids that are at home are coming with me. So I have dressed carefully putting on "my kids think I'm an ATM" tea-shirt.

Evening
Back home again and it didn't work the kids are now convinced that I am an ATM. The market cost me a fortune even though I bought very little the kids however (one aged 11 and the other aged 7) managed to buy lots and they assured me that everything they bought (or should I say I paid for) was really really important really dad or was it the tea-shirt.

Ah well time to feed the pigs again.

24 The baby, the shape box and the mallet

Having children has been a real blessing to me and I have learned lots of things through my children. Before he could talk my youngest son Rory had become my youngest ever teacher. It came about as many of these things do completely by chance. I was working with North Birmingham Mental Health Trust at the time and buzz phrases that were being bandied about like there was no tomorrow were "functional Teams" and Fidelity to the Model. What this in fact meant was that we followed strict entry criteria into a service for clients and that we did not deviate in anyway shape or form from the care pathway that was the driving force of the team.

My role was development work within one of the assertive outreach teams and I can honestly say that the team I worked with still remains one of the best teams I have ever had the pleasure to work with. On reflection it is clear to me that what made this functional team functional was that individually they were so dysfunctional that they had learned to support each other as much as they supported the clients. The biggest problem with this functional team and fidelity to the model approach was that it was clearly not working for many of the clients. Yes, we were reducing the length of stay and the amount of admissions to in-patient services but it seemed to us we were running a very expensive maintenance service and recovery was not even on the agenda. It is in this setting that Rory at his time all of a year and a bit of him decided it was time to start teaching dad some new truths about the world.

His favorite toy at this time was a shape box, you know the kind of thing I mean, it was a big square with holes that were shaped there were round holes, square holes, rectangular holes and pyramid shaped holes and there was also a number of spongy shapes that clearly fitted the holes and believe it or not a whole psychological theory that went with the box the holes and the shapes.

My favorite psychologist is a Russian guy (now long dead) called Lev Vygotsky his theories around child development explored how children cognitively developed understanding of how to work through the challenge that things like shape boxes presented to the child. He postulated that the child would initially attempt to put a shape through any of the holes in the box and if it did not fit the child would then move to the next hole and the next until the hole that the shape fitted in was found then the child would repeat this action and therefore learn the shape that matched the hole, they would then do the same with each shape until they learned them all. That was Vygotskys' theory unfortunately my son Rory was under two at the time and so had never read Vygotsky in fact he couldn't read at all. So as Rory faced the shape box dilemma (without the aid of Vygotsky) I was able to observe him and watch as he learned.

Like all babies Rory picked up a shape it was a square and then attempted to put it through the round hole of course it did not fit. Rory kept on trying to put the square into the circle getting more and more frustrated and angry as it refused to go in. His poor little face was changing color from pink to purple then blue he was so determined to make it happen. Just as I was about to intervene Rory put a hand behind him and picked up his mallet and before I could reach him he had struck the square peg as hard as he could and whoosh it went through the circle. Then there was silence both Rory and I looked at the shape box my mouth was wide open and then Rory looked at me a smile upon his face he then pointed to the shape box made some baby sounds that meant again.

Roll over Vygotsky

25 The Wizard of OZ

One of the most memorable things for me about my first admission as an involuntary psychiatric patient was meeting a self-professed male witch - an intimidating fellow patient who exerted dominance over others through use of fear.

Being the peace-loving, pacifist I am, it wasn't long after I was admitted we had a run-in with each other. I objected to his bullying tactics, and in a vocal confrontation I became angry with the guy. In fact, I was so angry that I slammed my fist on a table between us to emphasize my point. It was an overcast day.

Right at the precise moment I struck the table a bolt of lightening and thunder came from the sky. The witch cowered. Here was I this not so anymore skinny young bloke who was very angry and quite clearly had the power to command the heavens. Needless to say, he left me well alone for the rest of my stay in hospital!

26 An Anonymous Tip

When I was driving cabs earlier this year I picked up this gentleman from one of TSV's up market hotels. He was dressed in the normal psychiatrist clobber, bow tie, expensive suit, usual stuff, anyway driving to the airport the conversation turned to M.H and he mentioned that he was a psychiatrist in town on consultation

The conversation then turned to the DSM and he related to me that when he was studying to become a psychiatrist at university he and a number of other students were approached by the author of the DSM (he did mention the doctors name but I have forgotten it since) to ask a large number of both public and mh patients a series of questions over a lengthy period of time plus they were to be paid for their efforts.

After a short time students being students decided that asking all these questions was really taking up too much of their time (they could be doing far better things) so at one of their weekly reporting meetings they decided to make up the answers themselves (they were getting paid anyway).

That is how the DSM was born, my passenger promised me the story was absolutely true and so the DSM is based on falsely supplied replies.

Oh no the foundation of everything I believe has been shaken to the core, As If!

27 Turnaround

A driver is pulled over by a policeman. The police man approaches the driver's door. "Is there a problem Officer?" The policeman says, "Sir, you were speeding. Can I see your licence please?" The driver responds, "I'd give it to you but I don't have one." "You don't have one?" The man responds, "I lost it four times for drink driving." The policeman is shocked. "I see. Can I see your vehicle registration papers please?".

"I'm sorry, I can't do that. The policeman says, "Why not?" "I stole this car." The officer says, "Stole it?" The man says, "Yes, and I killed the owner." At this point the officer is getting irate. "You what?"

"She's in the boot if you want to see." The Officer looks at the man and slowly backs away to his car and calls for back up. Within minutes, five police cars show up, surrounding the car. A senior officer slowly approaches the car, clasping his half drawn gun.

The senior officer says' "Sir, could you step out of your vehicle please?" The man steps out of his vehicle. "Is there a problem sir?" "One of my officers told me that you have stolen this car and murdered the owner." "Murdered the owner?" The officer responds, "Yes, could you please open the boot of your car please?"

The man opens the boot, revealing nothing but an empty boot. The officer says, "Is this your car sir?" The man says "Yes," and hands over the registration papers. The officer, understandably, is quite stunned. "One of my officers claims that you do not have a driving licence." The man digs in his pocket revealing a wallet and hands it to the officer.

The officer opens the wallet and examines the licence. He looks quite puzzled. "Thank you sir, one of my officers told me you didn't have a licence, stole this car, and murdered the owner." The man looks straight into the officers' eyes and replies, "I bet you the lying bastard told you I was speeding, too!"

One Last Thought

I was once asked "How can I get myself out of the psychiatric system"? I pondered this question for a few moments then replied "Stop seeing a psychiatrist

Thanks for your time

Ron Coleman

May 2017

Printed in Poland
by Amazon Fulfillment
Poland Sp. z o.o., Wrocław